THE MASTERS OF
ENGRAVING AND
ETCHING

FOUR EARLY ITALIAN
ENGRAVERS

FOUR EARLY ITALIAN ENGRAVERS

ANTONIO DEL POLLAIUOLO / ANDREA MANTEGNA
JACOPO DE' BARBARI / GIULIO CAMPAGNOLA

BY TANCRED BORENIUS PH. D.

PROFESSOR OF THE HISTORY OF ART IN THE
UNIVERSITY OF LONDON

THE MEDICI SOCIETY LTD. 7 GRAFTON ST.
LONDON & 755 BOYLSTON ST. BOSTON. U. S. A.
1 9 2 3

PREFACE

The present volume is devoted to the four masters who, among the early Italian engravers known to us by name, easily come first in importance. In certain cases, the works of some anonymous followers of the masters in question have also been brought within the scope of the book.

Although the engravings of which this volume treats have long been eagerly sought after by collectors, it is by no means often that one comes across good and well-preserved impressions of these plates. Mutilations caused by ruthless trimming are of regrettably frequent occurrence; and in selecting specimens for reproduction, it is often very tantalising to decide between the rival claims of a good, but cut impression, and of a less good, but complete one. The locality of each impression reproduced in the present volume has been stated; it will be seen that it is geographically an extensive field that has been drawn upon.

Sizes are given in millimetres, height preceding width; whenever possible the dimensions of the plate are stated, otherwise the largest available dimensions of the engraved surface. The size given is not necessarily that of the specimen reproduced, and it is as well to emphasize that the shrinkage and expansion of paper cause all such data to be of a somewhat relative accuracy.

An attempt has been made to give a census of existing impressions of the engravings enumerated. The works of Dr. Kristeller and Prof. A. M. Hind have on this point rendered great service, though considerable amplification has been possible in many instances. It is chiefly public collections, and such private collections as are of a more permanent nature, that have been passed in review; collections that have ceased to exist have only been noticed to a limited extent. Absolute completeness is, of course, unattainable in a census of this character; one may get comparatively near to it in the case, say, of Giulio Campagnola, but again in the case of Mantegna and his school, for example, one necessarily can only register a small proportion of existing impressions. Nevertheless, it may be hoped that the census, such as it is, will prove useful; and in any case the net has been flung sufficiently wide to allow of inferences as to whether a given print is a rare one or not.

The author has received valuable and ungrudging assistance from a great many quarters. He is anxious to tender grateful acknowledgments to the numerous officials of Print Rooms and Museums in Europe and America who have courteously put him in possession of important information; and he would especially like to place on record the help in his work which has been afforded by Baron Edmond de Rothschild and Mr. Paul G. Sachs.

London, August 1923.

Tancred Borenius.

TABLE OF CONTENTS

VI

LIST OF ABBREVIATIONS

B. = Bartsch.   P. = Passavant.   K. = Kristeller.   G. = Galichon.
P. L. = Plate line.

When the name of a town only is stated, the reference is to the
principal public print collection in that city.

DRESDEN.   P. R. = Print Room.

          F. A. = Friedrich August II. collection.

LONDON.   B. M. = British Museum.

         V. & A. = Victoria & Albert Museum.

         R. A. = Royal Academy, Burlington House.

PARIS.   B. N. = Bibliothèque Nationale.

        Dutuit = Dutuit collection, Petit Palais.

    E. de R. = Baron Edmond de Rothschild collection.

VIENNA, Staatsb. = Staatsbibliothek, now amalgamated with the Albertina collection.

ZURICH.   Print Room of the Eidgenössisches Polytechnikum.

I. ANTONIO DEL POLLAIUOLO

INTRODUCTION

ANTONIO DEL POLLAIUOLO — painter, goldsmith, sculptor in bronze, and engraver — was born at Florence, probably in 1432, the son of a goldsmith. The earlier part of his career was spent in Florence; from about 1484 to his death, on February 8th, 1498, he was settled in Rome, where he produced, among other things, the bronze tombs of two Popes, Sixtus IV. and Innocent VIII. Much of his work was carried out in conjunction with his younger brother Piero (1443—1496).

In his art generally, Antonio del Pollaiuolo may be said to continue the tendencies of realism, of which earlier exponents at Florence, during the first half of the fifteenth century, were, in sculpture, Donatello, and in painting, Masaccio, Paolo Uccello, and Andrea del Castagno. According to Vasari (c. 1550) Antonio del Pollaiuolo acquired his knowledge of anatomy by dissecting human bodies; and the vivid realization of intense muscular tension is undoubtedly a central feature of his art, particularly apparent in his one great engraving, the *Battle of Naked Men*. His example in this respect meant much to later art — as witness, for instance, the work of Luca Signorelli and Michelangelo —; and a significant proof of his widespread influence as an interpreter of the nude is afforded by the fact that at least one cartoon of nude figures by Pollaiuolo belonged to Francesco Squarcione, head of the great fifteenth century art school in Padua, and teacher of Andrea Mantegna, and doubtless was one of the drawings which he used to put before his pupils to copy*.

Antonio del Pollaiuolo is known to have been associated in 1461—62 with Maso Finiguerra (1426—1464), a Florentine goldsmith, worker in niello and engraver, round whose name legend has been busy, but who may nevertheless be held, with considerable probability, to be the author of a number of Florentine engravings in what is known as the "Fine Manner", in which the shadows are crosshatched (as distinguished from the "Broad Manner" in which shading is done by means of parallel, *unconnected* lines). The one engraving which may confidently be given to Antonio del Pollaiuolo himself — the *Battle of Naked Men*, unquestionably one of the most astonishing productions of Italian Quattrocento art — occupies technically a place apart from these two groups inasmuch as shading here is done by means of parallel

---

* This cartoon ('unum cartonum cum quibusdam nudis Poleyoli') was lent by Squarcione to his pupil Marinello who failed to return it. See document of 1474, in Lazzarini and Moschetti, *Nuovo archivio veneto*, ser. ii. vol. xv. (1908), p. 117 et seq., 295.

1

lines *connected* by a return stroke: a technique similar to that of Andrea Mantegna. The date of this engraving must remain conjectural; but following Professor A. M. Hind we may put it about 1470 — perhaps later rather than earlier; and all things considered, it seems probable that it was Pollaiuolo's example which prompted Mantegna's adoption of this method of shading, and not the reverse.

Vasari mentions 'other engravings' as having been done by Pollaiuolo after the *Battle of Naked Men*. No such productions can, however, now be pointed out. Artistically, the *Battle of Naked Men* is so infinitely superior to the *Hercules and the Giants* and the *Two Centaurs fighting* formerly given to Pollaiuolo, as to make it impossible to regard them as being by the same hand. They must be considered as works of Pollaiuolo's school, the engraver of *Hercules and the Giants* actually, as it appears, working from a cartoon of Pollaiuolo's.

BIBLIOGRAPHY

BARTSCH, A., *Le Peintre Graveur*, vol. xiii. (Vienna, 1811), pp. 201—204.
CROWE, J. A., & CAVALCASELLE, G. B., *A History of Painting in Italy*, vol. iv. (1911, edited by L. Douglas, assisted by G. de Nicola), pp. 216—234.
CRUTTWELL, MAUD, *Antonio Pollaiuolo* (London, 1907).
HIND, A. M., *Catalogue of Early Italian Engravings preserved in the Department of Prints and Drawings in the British Museum* (London, 1910), pp. 189—194.
PASSAVANT, J. D., *Le Peintre-Graveur*, vol. v. (Leipzig, 1864), pp. 49 sq.

A. ANTONIO DEL POLLAIUOLO

Cambridge, Mass. (Mr. Paul G. Sachs)   415×613 mm

1. BATTLE OF NAKED MEN

B. 2.

Signed on the tablet on the left: OPVS ANTONII POLLAIOLI FLORENTINI.

The great majority of existing impressions of this engraving are of poor quality, having been taken after the plate had been considerably worn. The impression here reproduced is one of the finest known; another one of high quality is that in the collection of Prince Liechtenstein.

Vasari refers to the present engraving in the following passage (trans. by G. de Vere, iii. 241): "He had a more modern grasp of the nude than the masters before his day, and he dissected many bodies in order to study their anatomy. He was the first to demonstrate the method of searching out the muscles, in order that they might have their due form and place in his figures, and he engraved on copper a battle of nude figures all girt round with a chain"— the last statement apparently derived from the fact that the two standing figures in the centre foreground hold the ends of a chain.

COPIES: 1. Engraving, background blank, signed 'Opus Lucem Florentini Edinplesa in Stragua'.
          2. Woodcut, signed 'Johannes de Francfordia'.

5

IMPRESSIONS: *Amsterdam, Berlin, Boston (Mr. Francis Bullard), Bremen, Budapest, Cambridge, Mass. (Fogg Museum and Mr. Paul G. Sachs), Chatsworth, Dresden (P. R. & F. A. II), Florence (Uffizi and Marucelliana), Gotha, Hamburg, Prince Liechtenstein, London (B. M. and V. & A.), Manchester (Whitworth Institute), New York, Northwick Park, Oxford, Paris (B. N. and Dutuit), Pavia, Rome (Corsiniana and Vatican), Vienna (Staatsb. and Dr. Julius Hofmann. Sale, Boerner, 1922, No. 814), Zurich.*

B. SCHOOL OF POLLAIUOLO

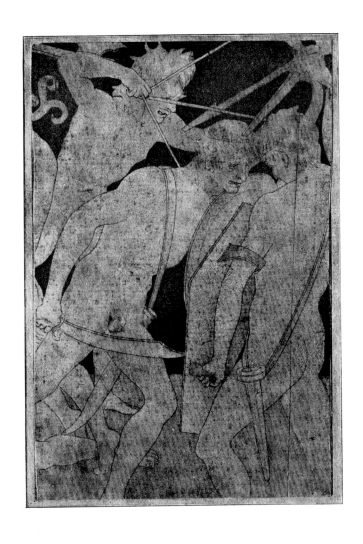

Fragment of the cartoon for the engraving of
HERCULES AND THE GIANTS
(Fogg Art Museum, Cambridge, Mass.)

London   369×554 mm

1. HERCULES AND THE GIANTS

B. 3

FIRST STATE: Shading of vines and wood in background not completed; no inscriptions.

SECOND STATE: As reproduced; the inscription below runs: QVOMODO HERCVLES
PERCVSSIT ET VICIT DVODECIM GIGANTES. The sword-sheath of
Hercules is inscribed HERCVLES.

There exists a fragment of a cartoon by Pollaiuolo (now in the Fogg Art Museum, at
Cambridge, Mass.) containing part of the four first figures in this composition, counting
from the right. This cartoon fragment was formerly in the collection of the Earl of
Pembroke at Wilton House (see S. A. Strong's publication of the Wilton Drawings, London 1900,
Part II, No. 17) and had at some time been retouched so as to conform more closely with
the present engraving. These later disfigurements have recently been removed, with the
happiest results. The cartoon is in the same direction as the engraving.

IMPRESSIONS: First state: *Chatsworth, London, Vienna (Staatsb.).* Second state: *Chatsworth,
Dresden, London (B. M. and late Morrison Collection, Sale, Sotheby's, May 1st, 1908, No. 106),
Vienna (Staatsb.).*

9

London   198×321 mm

2. TWO CENTAURS FIGHTING

B. xv. 478. 23 (as G. Reverdino). P. 4.

As pointed out by Prof. A. M. Hind, the two soldiers on the left correspond, in reverse, to those watching the Decollation of St. John the Baptist in a panel of the embroideries, designed by Antonio del Pollaiuolo in 1466 and now in the Museo dell' Opera del Duomo at Florence (reproduced in Maud Cruttwell, *op. cit.*, plate facing p. 114).

IMPRESSIONS: *Berlin, London, Paris (B. N. and E. de R.), Vienna (Staatsb.).*

II. ANDREA MANTEGNA

INTRODUCTION

A NDREA MANTEGNA, painter and engraver, was born, probably at Isola di Carturo between Padua and Vicenza in 1430 or 1431. He studied under the painter Francesco Squarcione at Padua and worked in the latter city up to 1460, when he entered the service of the Marquesses of Mantua, in which he remained till his death on September 13th, 1506. In 1488—90, he was lent to the Pope, for the purpose of decorating a chapel in the Vatican; and there is some, though not conclusive, evidence of a visit of his to Tuscany (Pisa) in 1467.

As an artist, Mantegna shows himself possessed by an absolutely romantic passion for the antique, for everything that savours of classical Rome. Stern and statuesque, his art is nevertheless full of tremendous vital and dramatic power; and certain of his works, like his engraving of the Virgin and Child and some paintings of the same subject (Accademia Carrara, Bergamo, Museo Poldi Pezzoli, Milan, and Kaiser Friedrich Museum, Berlin) reveal an exquisite and intense tenderness of feeling. The example of Donatello's sculptures, of which there were many in Padua, meant a great deal for the formation of Mantegna's style.

According to Vasari, Mantegna was prompted to take up the art of engraving, having become acquainted during his stay in Rome (1488—90) with "this thing" — which refers loosely to the alleged discovery by Maso Finiguerra of the art of engraving, and the work of the Florentine engraver Baccio Baldini. Little reliance can, however, be placed on this story, and we know for a fact that as far back as 1475 there were artists practising engraving at Mantua, with two of whom — Simone da Reggio and Zoan Andrea — Mantegna had a quarrel in that year. In treating of Antonio del Pollaiuolo it has been pointed out how Mantegna's method of shading with parallel lines, connected by a return stroke, was probably derived from Pollaiuolo: though it is hardly necessary to add that Mantegna would not be the great artist that he is if his methods did not bear a stamp of individuality. The whole question of the period covered by Mantegna's engravings is surrounded with uncertainty. That some of them belong to an early period of his career seems, however, certain; and a *terminus ante quem* for the dating of the *Bacchanal with Silenus* and the *Battle of the Sea-Gods* is supplied by the fact that two drawings by Albrecht Dürer, copied from these prints (now in the Albertina, Vienna) bear the date of 1494.

Adam Bartsch, writing more than a century ago, assigned to Mantegna himself no fewer than 23 engravings. Present day criticism, going by the criterion of artistic merit, acknowledges among these only seven as original works by the master, while most of the others, together with a number of kindred character, are grouped under the general heading "School of Mantegna". Mantegna's influence as an engraver no less than as a painter was very strong and widespread. Of some of the engravers imitating or copying him — e. g. Zoan Andrea and Giovanni Antonio da Brescia — we know authenticated works; but in endeavouring definitely to identify the authors of the engravings, gathered together under the above-mentioned general label, one generally encounters great difficulties.

BIBLIOGRAPHY

BARTSCH, ADAM, *Le Peintre Graveur*, vol. xiii. (Vienna, 1911), pp. 222—243.

CROWE, J. A., & CAVALCASELLE, G. B., *A History of Painting in North Italy*, edited by Tancred Borenius, vol. ii. (1912), pp. 1—44, 80—120.

DUPLESSIS, G., *Œuvre d'Andrea Mantegna reproduit et publié par Amand Durand*, Paris, 1878.

HIND, A. M., *Catalogue of Early Italian Engravings preserved in the Department of Prints and Drawings in the British Museum* (London, 1910), pp. 329—357.

KNAPP, F., *Andrea Mantegna*, 1910 (*Klassiker der Kunst*, vol. xvi.).

KRISTELLER, P., *Andrea Mantegna*, English edition, London, 1901. German edition, Leipzig, 1902.

LAZZARINI, V., & MOSCHETTI, A., "Documenti relativi alla pittura padovana del secolo XV" in *Nuovo archivio veneto*, ser. ii., vols. xv. and xvi. (Venice, 1908), (important for documents concerning Mantegna's early life).

PASSAVANT, J. D., *Le Peintre Graveur*, vol. v. (1864), pp. 73—79.

PORTHEIM, F., "Mantegna als Kupferstecher" in the *Jahrbuch der königlich preußischen Kunstsammlungen*, vol. vii. (1886), pp. 214—226.

YRIARTE, C., *Mantegna*, Paris, 1901.

A. ANDREA MANTEGNA

Munich   345×268 mm (P. L.)

1. THE VIRGIN AND CHILD

B. 8

The impressions of this engraving are as a rule more or less cut down: the example at Munich, here reproduced, though a late impression, is of interest as showing the plate line. A reproduction of the fine, but less complete impression at Chatsworth is appended. Rembrandt's pharaphrase of this engraving (in his etching *The Virgin and Child with the Cat,* 1654, Bartsch 63) is of interest as being one of many proofs of Rembrandt's close study of Italian art.

FIRST STATE: Without the haloes.
SECOND STATE: The haloes added (as reproduced).

IMPRESSIONS: First state: *Berlin, Bologna, London, Paris (Mr. W. Gay), Vienna (Staatsb.).* Second state: *Amsterdam, Berlin, Brunswick, Cambridge, Mass. (Fogg Art Museum), Chatsworth, Dresden (P. R. & F. A.), Hamburg, London, Munich, Oxford, Paris (B. N. and E. de R.), Rome (Corsiniana and Vatican), Stockholm, Vienna (Academy, Albertina and Staatsb.), Weimar.*

Chatsworth

1. THE VIRGIN AND CHILD
B. 8

Paris   327×450 mm

2. BACCHANALIAN GROUP WITH SILENUS

B. 20

COPIES: 1. Engraving, in the same direction, recognizable by details such as the absence of the three horizontal lines on the back part of the right cloven hoof of the satyr, standing to the right of Silenus and helping to support him (Bartsch, xiii. 250, 20, copy).
2. Engraving, reversed and considerably smaller than the original, signed "R. R." (Bartsch, xiii. 357, 2).
3. Small print in the niello manner (Dutuit, No. 330).
4. Woodcut copy (P. v. 77).

IMPRESSIONS: *Amsterdam, Berlin, Bremen, Brunswick, Budapest, Copenhagen (2), Dresden (P. R. and F. A.), Florence (Uffizi), Hamburg, London (B. M. [3] and V. & A. [2]), Manchester (Whitworth Institute), Munich, Oxford (2), Paris (B. N., E. de R. and Dutuit), Rome (Corsiniana and Vatican), Stockholm, Vienna (Academy, Albertina and Staatsb.), Weimar, Würzburg, Zurich (2).*

18

ANDREA MANTEGNA

Chatsworth   332×462 mm

3. BACCHANALIAN GROUP WITH A WINE-PRESS
B. 19

COPIES: 1. Engraving, in the same direction, recognisable by a number of minor details
(cf. reproduction, plate 23, in Hind's catalogue, Ottley. ii. 505).
2. Engraving in reverse (attributed by P. v. 77 to Zoan Andrea).
3. Etching, by Daniel Hopfer (B. 49).

IMPRESSIONS: *Amsterdam, Berlin, Bremen, Brunswick, Chatsworth, Coburg, Copenhagen (2), Dresden (P. R. and F. A.), Florence (Uffizi), Gotha, Hamburg, London (B. M., V. & A., Sir Philip Burne-Jones, Lucas Sale, Sotheby's, Nov. 8, 1922, No. 516), Manchester (Whitworth Institute, Munich, Oxford, Paris (B. N. and Dutuit), Rome (Corsiniana and Vatican [2]), Stockholm, Stuttgart, Vienna (Albertina and Staatsb.), Weimar, Würzburg, Zurich (2).*

ANDREA MANTEGNA

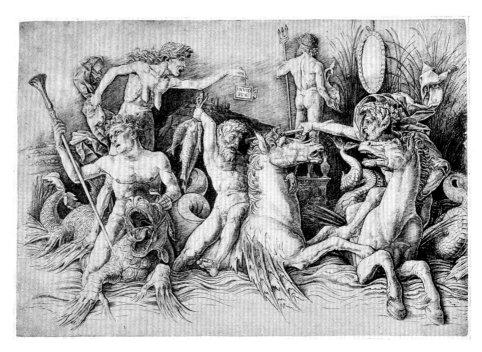

Boston   328×440 mm

4. BATTLE OF SEA-GODS
THE LEFT PORTION OF A FRIEZE
B. 18

The title "Battle of Sea-Gods" is consecrated by use (Vasari employs the expression *Battaglia de'mostri marini*). In point of fact, as demonstrated by Dr. Richard Förster (see *Jahrbuch der königlich preußischen Kunstsammlungen*, vol. xxiii, 1902, pp. 205 *et seq.*) the subject of this composition is derived from Diodorus Siculus Βιβλιοθήκη (of which the first translation into Latin was published at Bologna in 1472) which gives a long description of the habits of the strange people known as the *Ichtyophagi* or 'Fish-eaters'. In conformity with the view expressed by him in a letter to the Marquess of Mantua of November 28th, 1491 — 'it is the absolute truth, that envy always rules people of little consequence' — Mantegna shows these beings, who according to Diodorus are free from every passion, yet incited to fight by irresistible Envy, symbolized by the old woman standing on the back of the monster on the extreme left.

The original drawing by Mantegna for this portion of the composition is in the collection of the Duke of Devonshire at Chatsworth (reproduced in Kristeller, *Mantegna*, fig. 151); it is in the same direction as the engraving.

COPY: Etching by Daniel Hopfer (B. 47).

IMPRESSIONS: *Amsterdam, Bassano, Berlin, Boston, Bremen, Chatsworth, Copenhagen, Dresden (P.R. and F.A.), Florence, Hamburg, London (B.M. [2], V.&A., Sir Philip Burne-Jones and Lucas Sole, Sotheby's, Nov. 8, 1922, No. 515), Munich, New York, Oxford, Paris (B.N. and E. de R.), Rome (Corsiniana and Vatican), Vienna (Albertina and Staatsb.).*

20

Chatsworth
328×440 mm

5. BATTLE OF SEA-GODS
THE RIGHT PORTION OF A FRIEZE
B. 17

See the remarks on No. 4.

COPY: Etching by Daniel Hopfer (B. 48).

IMPRESSIONS: *Amsterdam, Basle, Berlin, Budapest, Chatsworth, Copenhagen (2), Dresden (P. R. and F. A.), Hamburg, London (B. M., V. & A. and Lucas sale, Sotheby's, Nov. 8, 1922, No. 515), Manchester (Whitworth Institute), Munich, New York, Oxford, Paris (B. N. and Dutuit), Rome (Corsiniana and Vatican), Vienna (Albertina and Staatsb.).*

Berlin   332×468 mm

6. THE ENTOMBMENT (HORIZONTAL PLATE)

B. 3

COPIES: 1. Engraving, in the same direction (cf. Hind, *op. cit.* p. 342).

2. Engraving, reversed, the o in the word *Redemptori* being smaller than the other letters used. (B. xiii. 296, 3, as Zoan Andrea).

3. Engraving, by Jean Duvet (B. 6) reversed, with various alterations and of smaller size.

4. Engraving, in the same direction, 18th Century, with monogram 'A. M.' and no inscription on the tomb. P. v. 76, copy C.

5. Small etching (cf. Hind, *op. cit.* p. 342).

6. Large 16th Century woodcut (cf. Hind, *op. cit.* p. 342).

IMPRESSIONS: *Amsterdam, Berlin, Bologna, Bremen, Brunswick, Budapest, Chatsworth, Copenhagen (2), Dresden (P. R. and F. A.), Edinburgh, Gotha, Hamburg, London (B. M., Sir Philip Burne-Jones and Mr. G. F. Hill), Madrid, Manchester (Whitworth Institute), Munich, New York, Oxford (2), Paris (B. N. and Dutuit), Parma, Rome (Vatican [2]), Stuttgart, Vienna (Albertina and Staatsb.), Zurich (2).*

22

Paris (Baron E. de Rothschild)   392×325 mm

7. THE RISEN CHRIST BETWEEN ST. ANDREW AND LONGINUS

B. 6

As regards the subject of this engraving it should be noted, that the most precious relic possessed by Mantua was that the Blood of Christ, supposed to have been brought by Longinus to Mantua, and enshrined under the high altar of the Church of S. Andrea in that city. 'One would be almost tempted to see in this composition the design for a group of statuary, perhaps for the high altar of S. Andrea' (Kristeller, *op. cit.* p. 402). Mantegna was buried in the same church.

23

COPY: Engraving, in the same direction with crosshatching, instead of parallel lines in the shading of the background (B. xiii. 318, 3, as Giovanni Antonio da Brescia).

IMPRESSIONS: *Amsterdam, Berlin (P. R. and late Davidsohn Coll.), Bologna, Bremen, Budapest, Cambridge, Mass. (Mr. Paul G. Sachs), Copenhagen, Dresden, Hamburg, London (B. M. [2], R. A., V. & A., Sir Philip Burne-Jones and Lucas Sale, Sotheby's, Nov. 8, 1922, No. 514), Milan, Munich, New York, Paris (B. N., E. de R. and Dutuit), Pavia, Rome (Vatican), Stuttgart, Zurich.*

B. SCHOOL OF MANTEGNA

SCHOOL OF MANTEGNA

Chatsworth   278×262 mm

1. THE TRIUMPH OF JULIUS CAESAR
THE ELEPHANTS
B. 12

This and the next number reproduce, in the direction of the original, the fifth and sixth
subjects in Mantegna's *Triumph of Julius Caesar,* a series of nine cartoons (or rather, tem-
pera paintings on paper, mounted on canvas) begun by the artist about 1485 and completed
(after an interruption in the work, during Mantegna's stay at Rome in 1488—90) by 1494.
These paintings — which form the most elaborate piece of archaeological reconstruction ever
carried out by Mantegna — were originally executed for the Castle at Mantua, where they
were used as stage decorations; they are now, in a terribly repainted condition, at Hampton

27

Court Palace, having been acquired by Charles I.*. The engravings show, however, certain variations from the form which the compositions had assumed in the finished paintings, and may possibly have been done from preliminary sketches: moreover, of one Triumph subject, which has been engraved, *The Senators* (see below No. 3), there exists no painted version at all.

* Compare E. Law, *Mantegna's Triumph of Julius Caesar*, London, 1921.

COPY: Engraving, in the same direction. B. xiii. 322, 8 (G. A. da Brescia).

IMPRESSIONS: *Amsterdam, Basle, Berlin, Bremen, Budapest, Cambridge, Chatsworth, Copenhagen, Dresden (P. R. and F. A.), Gotha, Hamburg, London (B. M. and Dr. Tancred Borenius), Madrid, Manchester (Whitworth Institute), Munich, New York, Oxford, Paris, Rome (Corsiniana and Vatican), Vienna (Albertina and Staatsb.), Washington, Weimar, Zurich.*

London   283×255 mm

2. THE TRIUMPH OF JULIUS CAESAR
SOLDIERS CARRYING TROPHIES
B. 13

COPIES: 1. Engraving, in reverse, with certain alterations: the shading of the background
extends across the whole plate, and the rendering of the trophies on the tray
is carried much further; also, a pilaster (closely akin to one by Zoan Andrea,
P. v. 83, 48) has been added on the right. B. xiii. 236, 14.

2. Engraving, in the same direction, but copied from (1). B. xiii. 322, 9 (Giovanni
Antonio da Brescia).

IMPRESSIONS: *Amsterdam, Basle, Berlin, Bologna, Bremen, Chatsworth, Copenhagen, Dresden
(P. R. and F. A.), Hamburg, London, Madrid, Munich, New York, Oxford, Paris (B. N. and Dutuit),
Rome (Vatican), Vienna (Albertina, Staatsb. and Staatsmuseum), Washington, Weimar, Zurich.*

Vienna   282×262 mm

3. THE TRIUMPH OF JULIUS CAESAR
THE SENATORS
B. 11

COPY: Engraving, in reverse. B. xiii. 321, 7 (G. A. da Brescia).

IMPRESSIONS: *Amsterdam, Basle, Bassano, Berlin, Bologna, Bremen, Brunswick, Chatsworth, Copenhagen, Dresden (P. R. and F. A.), Gotha, Hamburg, London, Madrid, Manchester (Whitworth Institute), New York, Oxford, Paris (B. N. and E. de R.), Parma, Pavia, Rome (Corsiniana and Vatican), Vienna (Albertina and Staatsb.), Washington, Weimar, Zurich.*

30

Cambridge, Mass. (Mr. Paul G. Sachs)   400×314 mm

4. THE SCOURGING OF CHRIST
WITH THE PAVEMENT
B. 1

In the specimen reproduced, a collector's mark is stamped upon the impression in the centre immediately above the lower border.
COPY: Engraving, in the same direction, the background behind one of the executioners being black, and the leg of the soldier seated on the left being encased in scaly armour. (Zani, *Enciclopedia*, ii. 7. p. 221; see also P. v. 75, 1.)

IMPRESSIONS: *Amsterdam, Berlin, Bremen, Brunswick, Cambridge, Mass. (Mr. Paul G. Sachs), Chatsworth, Copenhagen, Dresden (P. R. and F. A.), Gotha, Hamburg, London (B. M., R. A., V. & A., Sir Philip Burne-Jones and Lucas Sale, Sotheby's, Nov. 8, 1922, No. 512), Munich, Oxford, Paris (B. N., Dutuit and E. de R.), Rome (Vatican), Stuttgart, Weimar, Vienna (Albertina and Staatsb.).*

31

Hamburg   467×360 mm

5. THE SCOURGING OF CHRIST
WITH LANDSCAPE BACKGROUND
B. 1 (Copy)

The exact relation of No. 4 and the present engraving to one another is very difficult to determine. One may be copied from the other: or both may be derived from a common source, probably a drawing by Mantegna.

IMPRESSIONS: *Berlin, Dresden (P. R. and F. A.), Hamburg, London, Paris (B. N.), Rome (Vatican), Vienna (Albertina and Staatsb.).*

32

London 446×348 mm

6. CHRIST DESCENDING INTO HELL
B. 5

A picture by Marco Basaiti, based on this composition, is in the collection of Mr. F. N. Schiller of Esher House, Esher.

COPIES (in the same direction): 1. Engraving, Zani, *Enciclopedia,* ii. vol. 9, p. 63, A.
                                    2. Engraving, ascribed to Zoan Andrea.
                                    3. Engraving by Mario Cartaro (1566).

IMPRESSIONS: *Amsterdam, Berlin, Bologna, Bremen, Brunswick, Chatsworth, Copenhagen, Dresden, Gotha, Hamburg, London (B. M. [2] and V. & A. [2]), Munich, Oxford, Paris (B. N., Dutuit and E. de R.), Parma, Pavia, Rome, Stuttgart, Vienna (Albertina, Staatsb. and Staatsm.), Zurich.*

33

Chatsworth   450×362 mm

7. CHRIST TAKEN DOWN FROM THE CROSS

B. 4

FIRST STATE: No clouds in the sky; the branches of the tree in outline; no inscription
on the cross.
SECOND STATE: With the inscription INRI on the cross.
THIRD STATE: Clouds in the sky; the branches of the tree finished (as above).

IMPRESSIONS: First state: *Vienna (Albertina)*. Second state: *London (B. M. and R. A.),
Rome (Vatican)*. Third state: *Berlin, Chatsworth, Dresden (P. R. and F. A.), Hamburg, London,
Paris, Pavia, Vienna (Staatsb.)*.

Chatsworth   463×361 mm

8. THE ENTOMBMENT WITH THE THREE BIRDS
UPRIGHT PLATE
B. 2

COPIES: 1. Engraving, in reverse. B. xiii. 229, 2 (Copy No. 2).

2. Engraving, in the same direction, dated 1516 and without the inscription INRI on the cross. P. v. 75, 2, copy C.

3. Engraving, probably 18 th century, signed with a monogram 'A.M.' on the right.

4. Woodcut, reversed and modified in the Venetian edition of the *Meditazioni di S. Bonaventura* of 1500 (reproduced by Kristeller, *Archivio storico dell'arte*, ser. i., vol. v., 1892, p. 105).

IMPRESSIONS: *Berlin, Budapest, Chatsworth, Dresden (P. R. and F. A.), London (B. M. and V. & A.), Oxford, Paris (B. N. and Dutuit), Parma, Rome (Corsiniana), Stuttgart, Vienna (Staatsb.), Weimar.*

35

London   452×356 mm

9. THE EMTOMBMENT WITH THE FOUR BIRDS
UPRIGHT PLATE
B. xiii. 317, 2. (G. A. da Brescia).

By Zani and Passavant, the present engraving is looked upon as the original, and No. 8 as the copy. The question is extremely difficult to decide.
On the strength of the similarity of treatment, the present engraving may be assigned, as suggested by Prof. Hind, to the same artist as *Christ taken down from the Cross* No. 7.

IMPRESSIONS: *Amsterdam, Hamburg, London (2), Munich, New York, Paris (B. N. and E. de R.), Vienna (Albertina and Staatsb.).*

36

London   390×283 mm

10. THE ADORATION OF THE MAGI
'THE VIRGIN IN THE GROTTO'
B. 9

This engraving reproduces part of the central panel of the triptych by Mantegna in the Uffizi (No. 1111). Crowe and Cavalcaselle think the latter may date from 1464.

IMPRESSIONS: *Amsterdam, Basle, Berlin, Bologna, Chatsworth, Dresden (F. A.), London, Paris (B. N., Dutuit and E. de R.), Vienna (Albertina and Staatsb.).*

37

New York   350×255 (P. L.)

11. HERCULES AND ANTAEUS
B. 16

The plate of this engraving, judging from the many comparatively modern impressions, must have existed in recent times.

COPIES: 1. Engraving, in the same direction. By Giovanni Antonio da Brescia. B. xiii. 325, 14.
           2. Engraving, in the same direction, with additions. By Nicoletto da Modena. P. v. 77. 16 (copy).
           3. Etching, in reverse. By J. Hopfer. B. 25.

IMPRESSIONS: *Amsterdam, Bologna, Bremen, Cambridge, Mass. (Mr. Paul G. Sachs), Chatsworth, Coburg, Copenhagen, Dresden (P. R. and F. A.), Gotha, Hamburg, London (B. M. [2], V. & A. [2], and Lucas Sale (Sotheby's, Nov. 8, 1922, No. 514), Munich, New York, Oxford, Paris (B. N. and E. de R.), Parma, Pavia, Rome (Corsiniana and Vatican), Stockholm, Vienna (Albertina and Staatsb.), Weimar, Zurich.*

38

Cambridge, Mass. (Mr. Paul G. Sachs)   300×430 mm

16 AND 17. IGNORANCE AND MERCURY: AN ALLEGORY
OF VIRTUE AND VICE
(ONE COMPOSITION, CONSISTING OF TWO PLATES)

B. xiii. 303. 16. 17. (Zoan Andrea)

These two engravings form one continuous composition and are to be placed one above
the other.

They are intended as an elaborate allegory which, as explained by Dr. R. Förster (in the
Jahrbuch der königlich preußischen Kunstsammlungen, vol. xxii., 1901, pp. 78 et seq.) para-
phrases motives occurring in a passage of Galen's Προτρεπτικός, contrasting Mercury and
Fortune. In the upper portion, Ignorance, with some of the attributes of Fortune, is shown
enthroned on the globe on the right, between two allegorical figures; on the left a group
of four people, blind or blindfolded, are approaching the brink of a pitfall. In this atmo-
sphere of ignorance, Virtue does not thrive: so a laurel tree, symbolical of virtue, is shown

43

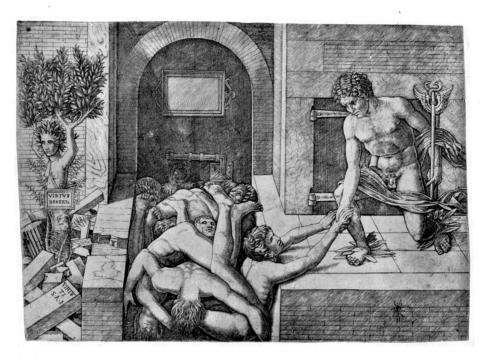

London   300×435 mm

on the right, burning — VIRTVS COMBVSTA as the inscription close by says. Below, we see the pit into which the blind have fallen, rescued by Mercury, the God of Invention: a Daphne figure on the left — virtue flourishing amid the ruins — bears the inscription VIRTVS DESERTA, and on the tablet in the foreground on the left is written "VIRTVTI S.A.I.", a cryptic phrase which is, however, fully explained by a sentence occurring twice in letters from Mantegna 'virtuti semper adversatur ignorantia'.

Mantegna's original drawing for No. 16 is in the British Museum.

COPIES: 1. Small engravings, in the same direction. Hind, *op. cit.* p. 354.
   2. Engravings, of the size of the original, 18th century, signed with a monogram 'A. M.' (B. xiii. 305).

IMPRESSIONS (No. 16): *Amsterdam, Berlin, Cambridge, Mass. (Mr. Paul G. Sachs), Hamburg, London (B. M. and V. & A.), Munich, Paris (B. N., Dutuit and E. de R.), Rome (Vatican), Vienna (Staatsb.).*

IMPRESSIONS (No. 17): *Amsterdam, Berlin, Hamburg, London (B. M. [2] and V. & A.), Munich, Paris (B. N., Dutuit and E. de R.), Vienna (Staatsb.).*

44

Vienna (Staatsb.) 230×92 mm

18. ST. SEBASTIAN

B. 10

IMPRESSIONS: *London, Paris, Vienna (Staatsb.).*

London   171×256 mm

19. SILENUS WITH A GROUP OF CHILDREN

B. xiii. 327 .17 (G. A. da Brescia)

Whether this engraving is copied after No. 20, or *vice versa*, is scarcely to be determined.

COPY: Etching by J. Hopfer, B. 28, either after this or the next number (reversing the present one).

IMPRESSIONS: *London, Paris, Vienna (Albertina and Staatsb.).*

London   164×237 mm

20. SILENUS WITH A GROUP OF CHILDREN

P. v. 82. 39 (Zoan Andrea)

IMPRESSIONS: *Amsterdam, London.*

Vienna (Staatsb.)   172×126 mm

21. THE MAN OF SORROWS

B. xiii. 296, 4 (Zoan Andrea)

Never before reproduced.

Compare the picture of the same subject by Mantegna (probably dating from about 1475) in the Gallery at Copenhagen (No. 200). The pose of the figure is reversed, there are considerable modifications in type of face and drapery, and the figures of the angels and the background are altogether different.

IMPRESSIONS: *Paris (B. N. and E. de R.), Vienna (Staatsb.).*

London   208×112 mm

22. THE MAN OF SORROWS

B. 7

Compare the picture of the same subject by Mantegna (probably dating from about 1475) in the Gallery at Copenhagen (No. 200). The face of Christ is somewhat different, the Angels are omitted and the landscape is altered.

IMPRESSIONS: *Hamburg, London, Paris, Vienna (Staatsb.).*

49

London   145×112 mm

23. HERCULES AND THE HYDRA

B. 15

From its similarity of technique, possibly the work of the same artist as the preceding number.

The proportions of the figure are reminiscent of the figure of Vulcan in the background of Mantegna's *Parnassus* in the Louvre (1497).

IMPRESSIONS: *Berlin, Budapest, Hamburg, London, Paris (Dutuit and E. de R.), Vienna (Staatsb.).*

50

London   117×171 mm

24. PORTRAITS OF LODOVICO GONZAGA AND HIS WIFE BARBARA OF HOHENZOLLERN

Duplessis, 25

Mantegna's great patron, Lodovico Gonzaga, Marquess of Mantua (1414—1478), and his wife Barbara of Hohenzollern (1423—1481), both appear in one of the master's frescoes in the Castle of Mantua, the figure of the Marchioness corresponding closely with the bust in the present engraving. A picture formerly at Hamilton Palace, and subsequently in the Cernuschi Collection in Paris (sold at the Cernuschi Sale, Paris, May 25 and 26, 1900, No. 53) is said to be similar to the present engraving, but not to be by Mantegna himself. On the strength of certain peculiarities of technique Prof. Hind (*op. cit.* p. 356) suggests that this engraving — which he considers is probably by the same artist as the next number — is the work of an eighteenth century engraver, pointing out in it an affinity to the manner of Francesco Novelli of whom we know that he, about 1800, was engraving after Mantegna, as was also one Antonio del Pedro; both working for Giovanni Maria Sasso who was collecting materials for a publication on the history of Venetian painting Other works of this class may be Nos. 25 and 26.

IMPRESSIONS: *Berlin (late Davidsohn coll.), London.*

51

London   246×266 mm

25. CHRIST IN HADES (FIRST PLATE)

B. xiii. 242. 1

The affinity to the engraving of the same subject, No. 6, does not go much beyond the figure of Christ. The composition may reproduce a design by Mantegna or an artist of his school: it also occurs in two pictures belonging respectively to the Pinacoteca at Bologna (No. 600, from the Zambeccari Collection) and the late Durazzo Collection at Genoa. As already recognized by Bartsch, the date of the present engraving is much later than that of Mantegna, and as Francesco Novelli (see previous No. 24) in a letter of his (Campori, *Lettere artistiche*, Modena, 1866, p. 325) mentions the Durazzo picture, it is a plausible suggestion that he engraved it.

Prof. Hind also refers to a drawing 'by some imitator of Mantegna' in the Bibliothèque Nationale, Paris (E. a. 31, rés.) which bears a relation to this and the next engraving.

IMPRESSIONS: *Berlin, London, Parma, Rome, Vienna (Albertina and Staatsb.).*

London   227×271 mm (P. L.)

26. CHRIST IN HADES (SECOND PLATE)

B. xiii. 243. 2

Contemporary with the previous number; the technique employed is in part etching.

IMPRESSIONS: *Berlin, Dresden (F. A.), London, Oxford, Parma, Rome, Vienna (Albertina and Staatsb.), Würzburg.*

53

London (Royal Academy)   157×138 mm

27. VIRGIN KNEELING, ADORING THE INFANT CHRIST

Hind, *B. M. Cat.* p. 588, No. 44

Although not showing the typical Mantegna technique of shading, this engraving (now for the first time reproduced) is brought into this context on account of its dependence on the central motive of a Mantegna composition of *c.* 1459, of which the finest version known is a picture in the collection of Mr. C. A. Rouse-Boughton-Knight, of Downton Castle, Ludlow (reproduced in Crowe and Cavalcaselle, *History of Painting in North Italy*, ed. Borenius, ii. 84 b).

IMPRESSIONS: *London (R. A.), Milan (Prince Trivulzio).*

54

III. JACOPO DE' BARBARI

INTRODUCTION

JACOPO DE' BARBARI was born probably about 1450. The name borne by him—though possibly as a sobriquet rather than as a family name strictly speaking—was that of an aristocratic Venetian family and a contemporary, and presumably relative, of his was one Niccolò de' Barbari, whose signature, accompanied by a trident, authenticates a picture of *Christ and the Woman taken in Adultery* now in the Palazzo Wallis-Mocenigo at Venice* — a work in which, however, scarcely any resemblance to the manner of Jacopo can be traced.

An Italian contemporary refers to Jacopo de' Barbari as 'Barberino of Venice who went to Germany and Burgundy and having adopted the manner of those countries did many things'. Between 1500 and 1508, Jacopo is recorded as working at various courts in Germany: his appointment as *'contrafeter und illuminist'* to the Emperor Maximilian I. dates from April 8, 1500, and during the next few years he probably chiefly resided at Nuremberg. He did undoubtedly come into contact with Albrecht Dürer during his stay in Germany, and may have met Dürer before in Venice; Dürer calls him in his writings *Jacob Walch* or *Meister Jacob*. In 1510 he is mentioned as painter to the Archduchess Margaret, Regent of the Netherlands, who in 1511, in consideration of the excellent services rendered by him and of his weakness and great age granted him a yearly pension of 100 livres for the remainder of his life. From the expressions used in this grant it seems natural to infer that Jacopo de' Barbari was then at least sixty years old; and this is the reason for putting the date of his birth about 1450. In 1516 he is mentioned as dead. A limited number of paintings by Jacopo de' Barbari has survived to the present day. One of them—a picture of an old man caressing a girl, formerly in the Weber Collection at Hamburg, and now in the John G. Johnson Collection at Philadelphia** — is the chief piece of evidence proving that the engravings which from their signature, the wand of Mercury, used to be given to the 'Master of the Caduceus', are by Jacopo de' Barbari: for the style of this work tallies exactly with that of the engravings in question and it is signed 'Ja. d. Barbari MDIII', the signature being accompanied by the Caduceus. It may not be out of place to mention that certain paintings which Morelli attributed to Jacopo de' Barbari — such as the *Portrait of a Youth* in the

* See for a reproduction of this picture, long thought to be missing, Dr. Geiger's paper, in the Berlin *Jahrbuch*, vol. xxxiii. (1912), p. 142.
** Reproduced in the Illustrated Catalogue of that collection (privately printed, 1913), vol. i. p. 350.

Vienna Gallery (No. 22) and the frescoes of the Onigo tomb in S. Niccolò at Treviso—are now universally recognised to be by Lorenzo Lotto.

In addition to the thirty engravings which can be regarded as works by Jacopo de' Barbari — all, with the exception of the *Sleeping Woman with a Snake* (No. 27), the *St. Sebastian* (No. 29) and the *Bust of a Woman* (No. 30), signed with the Caduceus — his *œuvre* includes the following woodcuts:

Battle between Men and Satyrs (K. 31, two plates).

Triumph of Naked Men over Satyrs (K. 32, three plates).

View of Venice, dated 1500 (K. 33, six plates). Published by Anton Kolb, a German merchant and acquaintance of Dürer's settled at Venice.

None of these woodcuts is signed.

Among the most striking features of Jacopo de' Barbari's style may be mentioned the drooping attitudes and languorous expression which he gives to his figures, and the long, softly gliding curves which predominate in his designs and seem a belated echo of Gothic art. His technique as an engraver has a very personal character, and has aptly been described as a transference to the plate of a fluent, slightly forceless pen drawing. None of his engravings is dated* and to give a chronological arrangement of them, based solely on criterions of style, is a very difficult matter. The classification of them which has been attempted in the following pages, is necessarily a tentative one, but brings nevertheless cognate examples more closely together than does the classification according to subjects, hitherto followed in all catalogues.

As will be seen from the notes on the single engravings, Jacopo de' Barbari has been frequently copied by German engravers and etchers.

BIBLIOGRAPHY

BARTSCH, A., *Le Peintre Graveur,* vol. vii. (Vienna, 1808), pp. 516—527 (as 'Le Maître au Caducée', among the early German masters).

CROWE, J. A. and CAVALCASELLE, G. B., *A History of Painting in North Italy,* edited by Tancred Borenius (London, 1912), vol. i. pp. 233—236.

GALICHON, E., 'Ecole de Venise, Jacopo de' Barbari dit le Maître au Caducée', in *Gazette des Beaux Arts,* ser. i. vol. xi. (Paris, 1861), pp. 311—319, 445—448.

GALICHON, E., 'Quelques notes nouvelles sur Jacopo de' Barbaris, dit le Maître au Caducée', ibid. ser. ii. vol. viii. (Paris, 1873), pp. 223—229.

HARZEN, E., 'Jacob de Barbary, der Meister mit dem Schlangenstabe' in *Archiv für die zeichnenden Künste,* vol. i. (Leipzig, 1855), pp. 210—220 (discovery of identity of Jacopo de' Barbari and the Master of the Caduceus).

HIND, A. M, *Catalogue of Early Italian Engravings preserved in the Department of Prints and Drawings in the British Museum* (London, 1911), pp. 442—457.

---

* Five of them (Nos. 1, 2, 17, 18, 19) were at one time pasted into a MS., now in the Munich Library, which is known to have been bound in 1504.

JUSTI, L., 'Jacopo de'Barbari und Albrecht Dürer' in *Repertorium für Kunstwissenschaft*, vol. xxi. (1898), pp. 346—374, 439—458.

KRISTELLER, P., *Engravings and Woodcuts by Jacopo de' Barbari*, International Chalcographical Society, 1896.

KRISTELLER, P., in Thieme-Becker's Dictionary of Artists, vol. ii. (Leipzig, 1908), *ad litt.*

MORELLI, G., *Die Galerien zu München und Dresden* (Leipzig, 1891), pp. 255—266.

PANOFSKY, E., 'Dürers Darstellungen des Apollo und ihr Verhältnis zu Barbari' in *Jahrbuch der preußischen Kunstsammlungen*, vol. xli. (1920), pp. 359 sqq.

PASSAVANT, J. D., *Le Peintre-Graveur*, vol. iii. (Leipzig, 1862), pp. 134—143.

THE VIRGIN AND CHILD WITH SS. JOHN THE BAPTIST
AND ANTHONY THE ABBOT
Painting by Jacopo de' Barbari in the Louvre

Vienna   189×122 mm

1. JUDITH

B. 1. G. 2. K. 1

COPIES: 1. Engraving, Angiolini Sale, 1895, No. 274.
2. Etching, by Jerome Hopfer (B. viii. 510, No. 20, together with *St. Catherine,* No. 2).
3. Engraving, in reverse, together with *St. Catherine,* No. 2. P. iii. 140, 25 (as original).

IMPRESSIONS: *Amsterdam, Berlin, Bremen, Dresden (P. R. and F. A.), Hamburg, London, Manchester (Whitworth Institute), Munich, Paris (B. N. and E. de R.), Vienna (Albertina, Staatsb. and Dr. Julius Hofmann, Sale, Boerner, 1922, No. 56), Zurich.*

Cambridge, Mass. (Mr. Paul G. Sachs) 181×118 mm

2. ST. CATHERINE

B. 8. G. 10. K. 10

COPIES: 1. Etching, by Jerome Hopfer, together with *Judith*, No. 1. B. 20.
2. Engraving, in reverse, together with *Judith* No. 1. P. iii. 140, 25 (as original).
3. Woodcut (K.).

IMPRESSIONS: *Amsterdam, Berlin, Cambridge, Mass. (Mr. Paul G. Sachs), Dresden (F. A.), London, Munich, Paris (B. N. and E. de R.), Vienna (Albertina and Staatsb.), Zurich.*

London   191×93 mm

3. THE REDEEMER

B. 3. G. 4. K. 7

IMPRESSIONS: *Amsterdam, Berlin, Dresden (P. R. and F. A.), London, Manchester (Whitworth Institute), Paris, Vienna (Staatsb.).*

London   117×100 mm

4. THE HOLY FAMILY

P. 26. G. 5. K. 4

Jacopo de' Barbari's picture of the Virgin and Child between St. John the Baptist and Anthony the Abbot, formerly in the Galichon collection and now in the Louvre (Grande Galerie, without number; see reproduction, p. 60) exhibits many analogies both with this engraving and *The Holy Family with St. Paul* (No. 12).

IMPRESSIONS: *Berlin, Dresden (F. A.), London, Paris (B. N. and E. de R.).*

64

London   228×167 mm (P. L.)

5. THE ADORATION OF THE MAGI

B. 2. G. 3. K. 2

In the composition—notably in the figures of the Virgin and Child and St. Anne—there lingers an echo of Giovanni Bellini's *Circumcision* of which the best known version (though not even that by the master himself) is in the National Gallery (No. 1455).

Dr. Kristeller has interpreted the subject of this engraving as *The Presentation in the Temple*; but on the whole Bartsch's title of the *Adoration of the Magi* seems preferable.

IMPRESSIONS: *Amsterdam, Berlin, London (B. M. and Lucas Sale, Sotheby's, Nov. 8, 1922, No. 503), New York, Paris, Vienna (Albertina).*

London   228×168 mm (P. L.)

6. SACRIFICE TO PRIAPUS
THE LARGER PLATE
B. 19. G. 21. K. 25

COPY: Engraving, in reverse, with variations, by Agostino Veneziano (B. 336).

IMPRESSIONS: *Amsterdam, Berlin, Bremen, Cambridge, Chatsworth, Coburg, Dresden (P. R. and F. A.), Hamburg, London (B. M. and Lucas Sale, Sotheby's, Nov. 22, 1923, No. 509), New York, Oxford, Paris (B. N. and E. de R.), Parma, Vienna (Albertina and Staatsb.)*

66

Vienna (Staatsb.)   137×196 mm

7. TRITON AND NEREID

B. 24. G. 17. K. 23

A resemblance between the head of the Triton here and in Dürer's engraving *The Seamonster* of about 1504 (B. 71) has been remarked.

COPIES: 1. Engraving, Italian, in reverse (K.).
          2. Etching, in the same direction, by Jerome Hopfer (B. 30).
          3. Engraving, in reverse, with variations, by Nicolas Wilborn (B. viii. 544, 4).

IMPRESSIONS: *Amsterdam, Berlin, Dresden, Hamburg, London, Munich, Parma, Vienna (Staatsb.).*

London   161×100 mm (P. L.)

8. APOLLO AND DIANA
B. 16. G. 16. K. 14

From this engraving Dürer in all probability derived the idea of his engraving of Adam and Eve of about 1505 (B. 68). An earlier stage in the evolution of that idea is seen in Dürer's drawing of Apollo and Diana in the British Museum (Lippmann, No. 233).

COPY: Etching, in the same direction, by Jerome Hopfer (B. 23).

IMPRESSIONS: *Amsterdam, Berlin, Dresden (P. R. and F. A), Florence, Hamburg, London (B. M. and Mr. G. Bellingham Smith), New York, Oxford, Paris (B. N. and E. de R.), Vienna (Albertina and Staatsb.), Zurich.*

68

London   160×100 mm (P. L.)

9. THREE NAKED MEN BOUND TO A TREE

B. 17. G. 26. K. 15

COPY: Etching, in reverse, by Jerome Hopfer (B. 39).

IMPRESSIONS: *Amsterdam. Berlin, Bologna, Bremen, Brunswick, Budapest, Cambridge, Coburg, Dresden (P. R. and F. A.), Florence, Hamburg, London, Manchester (Whitworth Institute), Munich, New York, Oxford, Paris (B. N. and E. de R.), Rome, Vienna (Albertina and Staatsb.), Zurich.*

London   140×194 mm (P. L.)

10. VICTORY RECLINING AMID TROPHIES

B. 23. G. 23. K. 27

COPY: Etching, in reverse, by Jerome Hopfer (B. 36).

IMPRESSIONS: *Berlin, Bremen, Copenhagen, Dresden (P. R. and F. A.), Hamburg, London (B. M. and Lucas Sale, Sotheby's, Nov. 8, 1922, No. 510), New York, Oxford, Paris (B. N. and E. de R.), Vienna, Weimar, Zurich.*

London   178×240 mm (P. L.)

11. THE VIRGIN AND CHILD

B. 6. G. 1. K. 3

Galichon's interpretation of the subject as Hagar seems unconvincing.

IMPRESSIONS: *Amsterdam, Berlin, Dresden, London (B. M. and Lucas Sale, Sotheby's, Nov. 8, 1922, No. 505), New York, Paris (B. N.), Vienna (Albertina and Staatsb.).*

71

Berlin   154×190 mm

12. THE HOLY FAMILY WITH ST. PAUL

B. 5. G. 7. K. 6

IMPRESSIONS: *Amsterdam, Berlin, Dresden, Florence, Hamburg, London, Paris, Rome, Vienna (Albertina and Staatsb.).*

72

Berlin   133×109 mm

13. TWO OLD MEN READING

B. 15. G. 25. K. 13

IMPRESSIONS: *Amsterdam, Berlin, London (B. M. and Lucas Sale, Sotheby's, Nov. 8, 1922, No. 507), Paris (B. N. and E. de R.), Vienna (Albertina and Staatsb.).*

Vienna (Staatsb.)   182×123 mm

14. VICTORY AND FAME

B. 18. G. 24. K. 26

A resemblance too definite to be accidental exists between this engraving and Dürer's *Four Naked Women* of 1497 (B. 75).

COPY: Engraving, in the same direction, by Nicolas Wilborn (B. 2).

IMPRESSIONS: *Amsterdam, Basle, Bremen, Dresden, London (B. M. and Lucas Sale, Sotheby's, Nov. 8, 1922, No. 508), Oxford, Paris (B. N. and E. de R.), Vienna (Staatsb.).*

London   130×164 mm

15. THE HOLY FAMILY WITH ST. ELIZABETH

B. 4. G. 6. K. 5

IMPRESSIONS: *Amsterdam, Berlin, Cambridge, Dresden (P. R. and F. A.), Hamburg, London (B. M. and Lucas Sale, Sotheby's, Nov. 8, 1922, No. 504), New York, Paris (B. N. and E. de R.), Vienna (Albertina and Staatsb.).*

75

Paris (Baron E. de Rothschild)   84×60 mm (P. L.)

16. ST. JEROME

B. 7. G. 8. K. 9

COPIES: 1. Engraving, in reverse (K.).
2. Engraving, in reverse, by Mathias Schmidt (Hind, *B. M. Cat.*, p. 450).
3. Woodcut (K.).

IMPRESSIONS: *Berlin, Bremen, London, Paris (B. N. and E. de R.), Vienna (Albertina and Staatsb.).*

London   85×43 mm (P. L.)

17. WOMAN AND CHILD WITH DISTAFF

B. 10. G. 28. K. 16

The affinity in general conception between this engraving and the next one, on the one hand, and Dürer's engraving *The Turkish Family* of *c.* 1495 (B. 85) is very striking.

COPIES: 1. Etching, in the same direction, by Jerome Hopfer, combined with a copy of *The Man with the Cradle* (No. 18) and an added dove above, the whole intended for a *Flight into Egypt* (B. 4).
2. Engraving, in reverse (Hind, *B. M. Cat.* p. 453).
3. Engraving, by Mathias Schmidt, 'inspecteur du Cabinet des gravures de Munich' (P. iii. 139).

IMPRESSIONS: *Berlin, London, Munich, Paris (B. N. and E. de R.), Vienna (Albertina and Oesterr. Museum).*

London   83×44 mm (P. L.)

18. THE MAN WITH THE CRADLE

B. 11. G. 27. K. 17

Dr. Kristeller reproduces a reversed version of this composition as the original.

COPIES: 1. Engraving, in the same direction (Hind, *op. cit.* p. 453).
        2. Engraving, in reverse (Hind, *op. cit.* p. 453).
        3. Etching, by Jerome Hopfer (see No. 17).
        4. Engraving, in the same direction, by Mathias Schmidt (P. v. 139).

IMPRESSIONS: *Berlin, Brescia (Martinengo Coll.), Dresden, London, Munich, Paris (B. N. and E. de R.), Vienna (Albertina and Oesterr. Museum).*

# JACOPO DE' BARBARI

London 84×61 mm (P. L.)

19. VENUS (OR VANITY)

B. 12. G. 14. K. 18

COPIES: 1. Engraving, in the same direction
2. Engraving, in the same direction, by Mathias Schmidt (P. v. 139).

IMPRESSIONS: *London, Munich, Oxford, Paris (B. N. and E. de R.), Vienna (Albertina).*

London   85×78 mm (P. L.)

20. A SATYR PLAYING THE FIDDLE

B. 13. G. 20. K. 19

An affinity of character with Dürer's engraving *The Satyr Family* of 1505 (B. 69) seems doubtless present.

COPY: Etching, in the same direction, by Jerome Hopfer (B. 32).

IMPRESSIONS: *London (2), Paris (B. N. and E. de R.), Vienna (Albertina).*

80

London   88×78 mm (P. L.)

21. A SATYR WITH A WINE-SKIN

B. 14. G. 19. K. 20

COPY: Etching, in reverse, by Jerome Hopfer (B. 31).

IMPRESSIONS: *Berlin, London, Paris (B. N. and E. de R.), Vienna (Albertina).*

London   98×112 mm (P. L.)

22. SACRIFICE TO PRIAPUS
(THE SMALLER PLATE)

B. 21. G. 22. K. 24

COPY: Engraving, in the same direction, and with some variations, by Nicolas Wilborn (B. 3).

IMPRESSIONS: *Amsterdam, Berlin, Chatsworth, Dresden, Florence, Hamburg, London, Paris, Vienna (Staatsb.).*

82

London   109×130 mm

23. A CENTAUR PURSUED BY DRAGONS

P. 30. G. 29. K. 21

ONLY KNOWN IMPRESSION: *London.*

London   102×117 mm (P. L.)

24. AN OLD WOMAN RIDING ON A TRITON

B. 22. G. 18. K. 22

IMPRESSIONS: *Amsterdam, Berlin, Bremen, Dresden, London, Munich, Paris, Vienna (Staatsb.).*

London   225×159 mm

25. THE GUARDIAN ANGEL

B. 9. G. 11. K. 11

IMPRESSIONS: *Amsterdam, Berlin, Bremen, Chatsworth, Dresden, London (B. M. and Lucas Sale, Sotheby's, Nov. 8, 1922, No. 506), New York, Oxford, Paris (B. N. and E. de R.), Vienna (Albertina and Staatsb.), Zurich.*

Vienna   297×180 mm

26. MARS AND VENUS

B. 20. G. 13. K. 12

IMPRESSIONS: *Amsterdam, Berlin, Coburg, Dresden, London, New York (Scholle Collection), Paris (B. N. and E. de R.), Vienna (Albertina and Staatsb.).*

Paris   181×117 mm (P. L.)

27. SLEEPING WOMAN WITH A SNAKE

P. 28. G. 12. K. 28

Interpreted by Passavant and Kristeller as Cleopatra, by Galichon as Ariadne. Jacopo de' Barbari's original drawing for this engraving (in reverse) is in the British Museum (reproduced by Kristeller, *op. cit.* p. 3).

IMPRESSIONS: *Berlin, London, Paris (B. N. and E. de R.), Vienna (Albertina), Zurich.*

Vienna (Staatsb.)   159×230 mm

28. PEGASUS

P. 29. G. 15. K. 29

COPY: Engraving, in the same direction, by Nicolas Wilborn (B. 5).

IMPRESSIONS: *Amsterdam, Berlin, Dresden, London, Manchester (Whitworth Institute), Munich, Paris (B. N.), Vienna (Staatsb.).*

London   212×151 mm

29. ST. SEBASTIAN

P. 27. G. 9. K. 8

IMPRESSIONS: *Amsterdam, Dresden (F. A.), London, Paris (B. N. and E. de R.), Vienna (Staatsb.).*

Berlin   337×264 mm

30. BUST OF A WOMAN

B. xiii. 103. 3. P. v. 225. 15. K. 30

Assigned by Bartsch to an anonymous author, and by Passavant to
Jacopo Francia.

IMPRESSIONS: *Berlin, Cologne, Dresden, Gotha, London, Paris (B. N.
and E. de R.), Stockholm, Vienna (Albertina).*

90

IV. GIULIO CAMPAGNOLA

INTRODUCTION

GIULIO CAMPAGNOLA was born at Padua about 1482, the son of Girolamo Campagnola, a distinguished writer and also an amateur painter. Efforts were made by Giulio's father in 1497 to obtain for him a situation at the Court of the Marquess of Mantua, so that he should be able to study painting under Andrea Mantegna; but this plan seems not to have materialised, as we in 1498 find him as one of the Court of Ercole I, Duke of Ferrara. He was still alive in 1515, since Aldo Manuzio, the famous printer, in his will of January 16 in that year, asked his executor to have a new italic type cut by Giulio Campagnola, but he died probably shortly afterwards. According to some recently discovered documents, he became a priest towards the end of his life.

Giulio Campagnola was a person of extraordinarily precocious development and marvellously many-sided gifts: painter, engraver, sculptor, poet, musician, scholar. So far, however, only one existing picture has in my opinion been coupled with Giulio Campagnola's name with any degree of certainty — *The Lovers and the Pilgrim*, an allegorical group, in the collection of Mr. R. H. Benson in London*.

Into the artistic constitution of Giulio Campagnola, receptiveness entered to a considerable extent. Dürer, Mantegna, Cima da Conegliano, and above all Giorgione may be mentioned as artists whom his works echo. Many of them have great attraction through the idyllic and romantic sentiment of which they are expressive.

Technically, Giulio Campagnola's engravings display in the majority of instances, a method of handling all his own, whereby dots and graver strokes are used in order to obtain delicacy and softness.

Only one of Giulio Campagnola's engravings is dated — the *Astrologer* (No. 10) of 1509.

In the following catalogue the engravings are grouped, not according to the subjects, but with a view to showing the gradual development of Giulio Campagnola's technique from pure line towards the utmost delicacy and atmospheric quality of minute wedge shaped strokes and dotting.

---

* See G. Fiocco, in *L'Arte*, vol. xviii. (1915), p. 150 *et. seq.* (with reproductions). Dr. Fiocco's case for ascribing to Giulio four frescoes in the Scuola del Carmine at Padua does not, however, seem to me to be made out.

BIBLIOGRAPHY

BARTSCH, A., *Le Peintre Graveur,* vol. xiii. (Vienna, 1811), pp. 368—376.

FLOCCO, G., 'La giovinezza di Giulio Campagnola' in *L'Arte,* vol. xviii. (Rome, 1915), pp. 138—156.

GALICHON, E., 'Ecole de Venise, Giulio Campagnola peintre-graveur du XVI. siècle'; in *Gazette des Beaux Arts,* ser. i. vol. xiii. (Paris, 1862), pp. 332—346.

HIND, A. M., *Catalogue of early Italian Engravings preserved in the Department of Prints and Drawings in the British Museum* (London, 1911), pp. 489—500.

KRISTELLER, P., *Giulio Campagnola,* Berlin, 1907 (Graphische Gesellschaft, V. Veröffent-lichung).

KRISTELLER, P., in Thieme-Becker's Dictionary of Artists, vol. v. (Leipzig, 1911), *ad litt.*

PASSAVANT, J. D., *Le Peintre-Graveur,* vol. v. (Leipzig, 1864), pp. 162—167.

VENTURI, L., *Giorgione e il Giorgionismo* (Milan, 1913), pp. 198—203.

94

Berlin   185×121 mm

1. THE PENANCE OF ST. CHRYSOSTOM

G. 4. K. 4

Copied in reverse from Dürer's engraving of the same subject
(B. 63, date prior to 1495).

IMPRESSIONS: *Berlin, Paris.*

Munich   81×111 mm

2. TOBIAS AND THE ANGEL

G. 1. K. 1

The landscape background is imitated in reverse from Dürer's *Little Courier* (B. 80, date prior to 1495).

As already noted by Dr. L. Venturi (*op. cit.* p. 200, n. 1), this engraving shows the influence of Cima da Conegliano (compare especially works like the *David and Jonathan* in the National Gallery and the two little *tondi* in the Gallery at Parma).

IMPRESSIONS: *Munich, Pavia.*

96

Paris (Baron E. de Rothschild)   107×136 mm

3. SATURN

B. 4. G. 5. K. 5

The landscape background is copied from Dürer's *Offer of Love* (B. 93, date prior to 1495); the stump of tree in the left foreground is borrowed from the same artist's *Little Courier* (B. 80, date prior to 1495).

IMPRESSIONS: *Paris (E. de R.), Pavia, Vienna (Albertina).*

London   136×123 mm (P. L.)

4. ST. JEROME

K. 15

IMPRESSIONS: *Frankfurt, Hamburg, London.*

London   167×123 mm

5. GANYMEDE

B. 5. G. 6. K. 6

The landscape is copied from Dürer's *Virgin with the Monkey* (B. 42, date prior to 1506).

FIRST STATE: The signature reads 'IVLIVS CAMPAGNOLA'.
SECOND STATE: The word 'ANTENOREVS' has been added to the signature.

IMPRESSIONS: First state: *Munich, Vienna.* Second state: *Amsterdam, Berlin, Dresden (F. A),
London, Paris (B. N. and E. de R.), Stockholm, Strasbourg, Vienna (Albertina).*

99

Naples   75×c. 116 mm

6. LANDSCAPE
(FRAGMENT)
K. 18

Copied with variations and on a bigger scale from a passage in the background of Dürer's *Sea-Monster* (B. 71, c. 1504). Obviously a fragment of the landscape background of some larger composition.

ONLY KNOWN IMPRESSION: *Naples.*

100

Paris (Baron E. de Rothschild)　　　　　　　　　　　　　　19×133—136 mm

7. THE OLD SHEPHERD

G. 12. K. 12

The group of houses in the background occurs also in Mr. R. H. Benson's picture *The Lovers and The Pilgrim*, which may be reasonably ascribed to Giulio Campagnola (see Fiocco in *L'Arte*, vol. xviii. (1915), p. 150 *et seq.*).

COPIES: 1. Engraving, in the same direction, by Agostino Veneziano (signed A. V.) B. 408. G. 12 copy 1.
　　　　2. Engraving, reversed, G. 12 copy 2, B. 7 (as original).
　　　　3. Engraving, reversed, with considerable alterations, by Agostino Veneziano (signed, in capitals, 'AGVSTINO DI MVSI' — G. copy 3).

IMPRESSIONS: *Cambridge, Mass. (Mr. Paul G. Sachs), London, Munich, Oxford, Paris (B. N. and E. de R.), Wolfegg (2 impressions).*

Berlin

130×185 mm

8. CHRIST AND THE WOMAN OF SAMARIA

B. 2. G. 2. K. 2

FIRST STATE: As reproduced above.

SECOND STATE: The plate has been damaged notably on the right of the tower in the background.

IMPRESSIONS. First state: *Berlin, Bremen, Brussels, Dresden (P. R. and F. A), Prince Liechtenstein, New York, Paris, Parma, Prague (late Lanna coll.), Vienna (Staatsb.).* Second state: *Chantilly, Copenhagen, Hamburg, London, Manchester (Whitworth Institute), Munich, Paris (Dutuit and E. de R.), Vienna (Albertina and Oesterr. Museum), Zurich.*

102

London   135×178 mm

9. THE YOUNG SHEPHERD

B. 6. G. 8. K. 8

FIRST STATE: In pure outline.
SECOND STATE: Minute wedge shaped strokes and dotting added (as reproduced above).

COPIES: 1. Engraving, in the same direction, without the head of the old man. By
         Agostino Veneziano (signed A. V.). B. 458.
         2. Engraving, in reverse.

IMPRESSIONS: First state: *London.* Second state: *Bologna, Frankfurt, London, Munich,
Paris (E. de R.), Vienna (Albertina), Wolfegg.*

103

London   98×153 mm

10. THE ASTROLOGER

B. 8 (Copy C). G. 11. K. 11

FIRST STATE: Pure line work, no inscription.
SECOND STATE: Dotted work, no inscription (as above).
THIRD STATE: Inscribed 'Ludovicus Longus Matheseos professor'. The date on the globe altered from 1509 to 1569; above, on the right, the figures '193'.

COPIES: 1. Engraving, in the same direction, by Agostino Veneziano (signed A.V.). B. 411. G. 11 copy 1. On the globe the figures 21, 40, 43, 50 and 1514.
2. Engraving, in the same direction, 13 windows in the building in the background instead of 14. G. 11 copy 2.
3. Engraving, reversed, with the date 1514 and the figures 40, 21, 50, 43 on the globe. G. 11 copy 3. B. 8 copy A.
4. Engraving, reversed, with the date 1509 and the figures 40, 21 (the 2 reversed), 50, 43 on the globe. G. 11 copy 4. B. 8 (as original).
5. Woodcut, on the title page of the book: Albohasen Haly, *De Juditiis astrorum* (Venice 1521).

IMPRESSIONS: First state: *Berlin.* Second state: *Bremen, Dresden (F. A.), Frankfurt, Hamburg, London, Munich, Paris (B. N. and E. de R.), Parma, Wolfegg.* Third state: *Berlin, Hamburg, Parma.*

104

Cambridge, Mass. (Mr. Paul G. Sachs)   345×237 mm

11. ST. JOHN THE BAPTIST

B. 3. G. 3. K. 3

Signed above on the left: IVLIVS CAMPAGNOLA · F· Below in the right hand corner the address: *Appresso Nicolo Nelli in Venetia.*

According to Prof. Hind (*op. cit.* p. 494) in some (apparently later) impressions, the word 'Appresso' in the address is spelt 'appresso'.

Girolamo Mocetto's engraving *St. John the Baptist* (B. 5) shows practically the same figure, only in reverse. Both engravings possibly go back to a common source — presumably a drawing by Mantegna.

105

Two drawings — one in the Louvre, the other in the Ambrosiana at Milan (reproduced in *L'Arte,* viii. 1905, pp. 250, 251) — which have been regarded as studies for this engraving are probably both copies.

IMPRESSIONS: *Amsterdam, Basle, Berlin (P. R. and late Davidsohn coll.), Bologna, Bremen, Budapest, Cambridge, Mass. (Mr. Paul G. Sachs), Dresden (P. R. and F. A.), Florence, Frankfurt, Prince Liechtenstein, London (B. M. [2], Miss Evelyn Brooke and Lucas Sale, Sotheby's, Nov. 8, 1922, No. 511), Manchester (Whitworth Institute), New York, Paris (B. N., Dutuit and E. de R.), Venice (Museo Civico), Vienna (Albertina and Staatsb.), Wolfegg.*

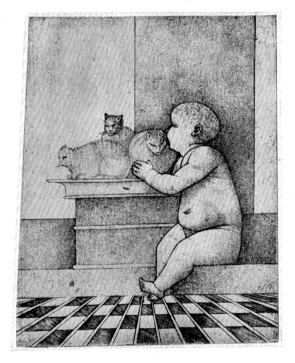

London   85×65—70 mm

12. CHILD WITH THREE CATS

G. 7. K. 7

ONLY IMPRESSION KNOWN: *London* (to its pedigree, as given by
Hind, *B. M. Cat.*, p. 495 may be added W. Esdaile collection: see initials
'W. E.' written on step, below on the right, and Esdaile sale catalogue,
June 27, 1840, Christie's, No. 291).

Dresden   119×181 mm

13. ALLEGORY: TWO NAKED WOMEN, BIRTH AND DEATH

K. 17

Copied in reverse from the engraving by Ludwig Krug (B. 11). The letters in the second and third states were added later.

FIRST STATE: Without a monogram.
SECOND STATE: With the letter L below on the left.
THIRD STATE: With a monogram HFP below on the left (as reproduced above).

IMPRESSIONS: First state: *Paris.* Second state: *Dresden.* Third state: *Dresden.*
Dr. Kristeller also mentions an impression (state?) in the collection of Count Stroganoff in Rome.

108

London   120×180 mm (P. L.)

14. WOMAN RECLINING IN A LANDSCAPE

G. 13   K. 13

FIRST STATE: As above.
SECOND STATE: Lines scratched across the plate.

IMPRESSIONS: First state: *Cambridge, Mass. (Mr. Paul G. Sachs), London, Paris (B. N. and E. de R.), Vienna, Wolfegg.* Second state: *Copenhagen.*

109

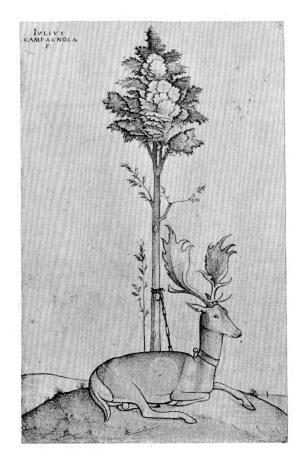

London   182×118 mm

15. STAG AT REST CHAINED TO A TREE
G. 14. K. 14

The stag seems copied from that on the back of a double portrait in the Liechtenstein
Collection, ascribed to Antonello da Messina (reproduced in Venturi, *Storia dell' arte italiana*,
vol. vii. pt. iv. p. 47). This picture was in 1567 in the collection of Gabriele Vendramin at
Venice and at that time assigned to Giovanni Bellini (see A. Ravà in *Nuovo Archivio
Veneto*, nuova serie, vol. xxxix. p. 159 *et seq.*).

It may be mentioned that the 'White Hart at Rest' was a favourite emblem in mediæval
symbolism: it was constantly used by Richard II. of England and is even painted at the
back of the Wilton Diptych.

IMPRESSIONS: *London, Paris (E. de R.), Vienna (Albertina).*

110

London   132—135×258 mm (P. L.)

16. SHEPHERDS IN A LANDSCAPE

B. 9. G. 9. K. 9

This engraving is the work of two hands: the major portion, which extends from the right border to about the summit of the mountain in the distance (or about as much as is reproduced in the first state of the copy described below) is by Giulio: the remainder shows the manner of his pupil Domenico Campagnola.

A sheet of studies by Giulio Campagnola for this engraving is in the Louvre (reproduced in Kristeller, *op. cit.* plates xviii. and xxiv.).

COPY: Engraving, reversed. First state: Uncompleted, showing only the right half of the composition. Second state: Completed, with changes, including the introduction of two cows from Marcantonio's *Judgment of Paris* (B. 245) into the background. Kristeller, *Giulio Campagnola,* p. 19.

IMPRESSIONS: *Amsterdam, Berlin (P. R. and late Davidsohn coll.), Bremen, Budapest, Cambridge, Chatsworth, Dresden (F. A.), Prince Liechtenstein, London (2), Munich, New York, Paris (B. N., Dutuit and E. de R.), Prague (late Lanna Coll.), Vienna (Albertina and Staatsb.).*

111

GIULIO CAMPAGNOLA

Dr. Kristeller also assigns to Giulio Campagnola two engravings of which he recollects seeing one copy each, though he has not been able to trace them again, *viz.*

THE PENANCE OF ST. CHRYSOSTOM

K. 19.   142×115 mm

"A nude woman, seen from behind, sits on the left, half turned to the right, on a cloth and holds a child in her right arm. Her hair is contained in a sack-like net. She looks towards the left, where a man is crawling on the ground. On the left, a tree and hill with shrubs, further back buildings, behind which, in the centre, rises a high rock."

IMPRESSION: *Prince Liechtenstein.*

LANDSCAPE WITH A SHEPHERD AND A WOMAN PLAYING THE FLUTE

K. 20

IMPRESSION: *Budapest.*

Two engravings — *Youth seated contemplating a skull* (G. 10, K. 10) and *Leda and the Swan* (K. 16) — I, in agreement with Prof. Hind, am not prepared to accept as works by Giulio Campagnola.

112

KEYS TO THE NUMBERS OF OTHER CATALOGUES

A dash indicates that the engraving in question by general consent is now excluded from the subject-matter covered by this volume.

ANTONIO DEL POLLAIUOLO

Bartsch	Present volume
1	School of Mantegna . . 12
2	Pollaiuolo 1
3	School of Pollaiuolo . . 1

ANDREA MANTEGNA

Bartsch	Present volume	Bartsch	Present volume
1	School of Mantegna . . . 4	14	School of Mantegna 2, copy 1
2	School of Mantegna . . . 8	15	School of Mantegna . . . 23
3	Mantegna 6	16	School of Mantegna . . . 11
4	School of Mantegna . . . 7	17	Mantegna 5
5	School of Mantegna . . . 6	18	Mantegna 4
6	Mantegna 7	19	Mantegna 3
7	School of Mantegna . . . 22	20	Mantegna 2
8	Mantegna 1	21	—
9	School of Mantegna . . . 10	22	—
10	School of Mantegna . . . 18	23	—
11	School of Mantegna . . . 3	Addition 1 .	School of Mantegna . . . 25
12	School of Mantegna . . . 1	Addition 2 .	School of Mantegna . . . 26
13	School of Mantegna . . . 2		

JACOPO DE'BARBARI

Bartsch	Present volume	Galichon	Present volume	Kristeller	Present volume
1	1	1	11	1	1
2	5	2	1	2	5
3	3	3	5	3	11
4	15	4	3	4	4
5	12	5	4	5	15
6	11	6	15	6	12
7	16	7	12	7	3
8	2	8	16	8	29
9	25	9	29	9	16

JACOPO DE'BARBARI (continued)

Bartsch	Present volume	Galichon	Present volume	Kristeller	Present volume
10	17	10	2	10	2
11	18	11	25	11	25
12	19	12	27	12	26
13	20	13	26	13	13
14	21	14	19	14	8
15	13	15	28	15	9
16	8	16	8	16	17
17	9	17	7	17	18
18	14	18	24	18	19
19	6	19	21	19	20
20	26	20	20	20	21
21	22	21	6	21	23
22	24	22	22	22	24
23	10	23	10	23	7
24	7	24	14	24	22
	—	25	13	25	6
	—	26	9	26	14
	—	27	18	27	10
	—	28	17	28	27
	—	29	23	29	28
	—		—	30	30

GIULIO CAMPAGNOLA

Bartsch	Present volume	Galichon and Kristeller	Present volume	Galichon and Kristeller	Present volume
1	—	1	2	12	7
2	8	2	8	13	14
3	11	3	11	14	15
4	3	4	1		
5	5	5	3	Kristeller	
6	9	6	5	15	4
7	7, copy 2	7	12	16	—
8	10, copy 4	8	9	17	13
9	16	9	16	18	6
		10	—	19	112
		11	10	20	112

THE MASTERS OF ENGRAVING & ETCHING

This Series is designed to enable Students and Collectors to obtain all the available knowledge in the smallest possible compass relating to the engravings and etchings of the recognised Masters from the earliest times.

Every known work by each Engraver is illustrated, thus obviating long, difficult and sometimes misleading descriptions.

The following works in the same Series as this Volume are either published or in preparation:

Albrecht Altdorfer. By EMIL WALDMANN, Director of the Kunsthalle, Bremen.

Marcantonio. By TANCRED BORENIUS.

Albrecht Dürer. By CAMPBELL DODGSON, Keeper of Prints and Drawings, British Museum.

Other Volumes are in active preparation